CRASH'S LAW

T H E   N A T I O N A L   P O E T R Y   S E R I E S

The National Poetry Series was established in 1978 to publish five collections of poetry annually through five participating publishers. The manuscripts are selected by five poets of national reputation. Publication is funded by James A. Michener, the Copernicus Society of America, Edward J. Piszek, the Lannan Foundation, the National Endowment for the Arts, and the Tiny Tiger Foundation.

1 9 9 5   C O M P E T I T I O N   W I N N E R S

Heather Allen, *Leaving a Shadow*
Selected by Denise Levertov, published by Copper Canyon Press

Marcus Cafagna, *The Broken World*
Selected by Yusef Komunyakaa, published by University of Illinois Press

Daniel Hall, *Strange Relation*
Selected by Mark Doty, published by Viking Penguin Press

Juliana Spahr, *Response*
Selected by Lyn Hejinian, published by Sun & Moon Press

Karen Volkman, *Crash's Law*
Selected by Heather McHugh, published by W. W. Norton

WINNER OF THE 1995

KAREN VOLKMAN

crash's LAW

poems

W. W. NORTON & COMPANY • NEW YORK • LONDON

NATIONAL POETRY SERIES

For information about permission to reproduce selections from
this book, write to Permissions, W. W. Norton & Company, Inc.,
500 Fifth Avenue, New York, NY 10110.

The text of this book is composed in Electra
  with the display set in Frutiger Black Condensed.
Composition by PennSet, Inc.
Manufacturing by Courier Companies, Inc.
Book design by Beth Tondreau Design / Robin Bentz
Title page and part opener art by Alexandra Exter: Sketch of Stage Construction,
Satanic Ballet, 1922. Courtesy of State Central Theatrical Museum, Moscow.

LIBRARY OF CONGRESS CATALOGING-IN-PUBLICATION DATA
Volkman, Karen.
    Crash's law : poems / Karen Volkman.
        p. cm.
    "Winner of the 1995 national poetry series."
    ISBN 0-393-03956-0
    I. Title.
    PS3572.O3947C73   1996
    811'.54—dc20   95-42534

W. W. Norton & Company, Inc., 500 Fifth Avenue, New York, N.Y. 10110
http://web.wwnorton.com
W. W. Norton & Company Ltd., 10 Coptic Street, London WC1A 1PU

1 2 3 4 5 6 7 8 9 0

CONTENTS

ACKNOWLEDGMENTS

Thanks to the National Endowment for the Arts,
the MacDowell Colony, and Yaddo for their support.

And to the many friends who have read these poems.

And to the editors of the following journals in which
some of these poems first appeared:

American Poetry Review: "The Gold Book"
The Boston Review: "Seasonal"
Chelsea: "Chemistry," "Infernal"
The Harvard Review: "Scarecrow"
The Paris Review: "The Case," "Chronicle,"
    "Equations," "Looking Back," "Persephone at Home"
The Partisan Review: "Tulips"
Poetry: "Casanova in Love," "From Shore"
Prairie Schooner: "The Pregnant Lady Playing Tennis"
Tar River Poetry: "Evening"
Western Humanities Review: "Daffodils," "Reflections,"
    "No Regrets," "Shipwreck Poem," "White Lily"

"The Case" was selected for *Best American Poetry* 1996
    (Adrienne Rich, guest editor)

And to Rick Meier, for much and more.

The Zeroes—taught us—Phosphorus—
We learned to like the Fire

EMILY DICKINSON

I.

Is it better to die by the hand of an intimate
or to die by the hand of a stranger?

The one with his pitchfork and the one with a wing of sorrow
and the one with a shaky plow.

The revenant sprawls by the pool
assessing opulent stucco and glossy indigo.

Planning new calamities for sad girls at the beach house,
their tan lines a testament to self-invention.

It is Miami in the world and in the mind,
the antique candy-striped umbrellas give no protection.

The tourists on Biscayne Boulevard
brandish cameras between pink and green hotels.

On the jetty, in spectral sunlight, in view of lovers, a pelican
swallows heart-shaped fishes one by one.

The time her lover hit her and she ran crying to the door
he said don't run out in the dark, he said I'll drive you.

In traffic, the shunt and pull
of engines, exhaust like cirrus scudding earth only lighter.

Where the freeway leaps impossibly skyward
like an inexpressible sentiment (I miss you).

—Packing to ship to the grandkids back east
six varieties of citrus.

The revenant as though he kept secrets
behind sunglasses takes the amnesiac waters.

Sun, triumphant, muscled between clouds,
heat for a moment the nearness we weep for.

I stay close to the water,
you stay close to the shore.

We forgot our coats, shoes,
left everything in a jumble,
stumbling barefoot on the rutted plain,
the blunt heat pressing at our necks
like an anxious question.

I loved my garden.
Loved the fat diameter
of the cow's girth, her somber lowing,
the soft scuff of my daughters' footsteps
on the bare swept floor,

our littered streets, the carters' cries
near the ramparts
strident at dawn. Was it
for this then? For *sin?*
For living? Were my herbs
leafy idols, calamitous

in their dainty pots?
Was it for this
they scourged us,
those keepers of abstraction
staunch in a gauzy heaven,
because we loved

inexpertly, inaccurately,
what would not stay?
All smoky diadems,
that ephemera.
I saw it.

I have no hands now
to touch or take.
I am all eye.
Memory and motionless witness
and salt my substance

preserves and keeps,
preserves and keeps —
and over everything
the unsmiling white faces, repeating
for goodness, for goodness, for goodness.

Never mind the climate. The gladiolas open up with the intelligence of bellwethers, a precise bruise on a wry face, unsmiling. It is the seemliest season, palm turned up for change. Do we take this greeting to mean *we are waiting* or *fortune is as fortune does (says the gravedigger to the worm)*?

Inside, the chandelier has accomplished its usual transformation, in triumph over the time change. Outside: natural causes over systematized violence, a twilight at a time. I give up ghosts one by one, kissing them with a restraint palpably domestic. Each is different, though, and wears a watch, whose intricate, delicate innards are beginning to rust.

THE RED SHOES

Not red, she said, but the dark
of pure desire, as bright and private
as the space beneath the ribcage.
They shine! said the blind old woman.
Yes, they shine.

　　In Denmark, it is always snowing.
　　The blond hair of the natives
　　curls like Qs on their sensible foreheads.

She'd learned her Latin and piano.
Learned *tibia fibula femur* with a tutor.
Till the bad old days of hunger were forgotten
in jewels and balls and gowns. (Starvation
brings you closer to the privacy of bones.)

　　It is Denmark, it is snowing.
　　The ice-fish take their blindness
　　from the ice.

Believing in distance, one learns to dance.
(But in a colder bed, the old woman
is dying.) Believing in passion
and the touch of the prince. (Or in
cranium mandible clavicle sternum.)

And later, by the frozen lake,
the voice of the ax-man,
familiar, whispering,
My sweet
ballerina, when are you going to learn?

If the impersonal made personal isn't personal, then what is there?

Removing one's trousers, as one acquires a taste.

Do you prefer the sheets with the frilly edges or the black ones?

Inspected, adjusted, apprehended, overcome.

Shall I tell you a story of origins, dull and fatal?

In the beginning, a fracture (as one acquires a taste).

Shall I tell you of near escapes, with a punch line?

Sitting, or standing up?

A bastard and a fool go to market with a crate of pigeons.

I evade my history as one favors a damaged limb.

In the attendant pleasure, regardless.

Do you prefer the sheets with the maroon Vesuvius or floral print?

In the beginning, a tremor (as one remembers a face).

If you lose the will to imagine another's mind, then what is there?

Unbuttoning one's blouse, as one renounces a faith.

The sheets with the slag heap or with the map of starry vistas?

And your blue eyes transparent in lamplight.

Standing, or lying down?

(As one inhabits a secret.)

The fool says to the bastard, You mean they fly too?

EQUATIONS

The moon isn't looking for solutions.
She's grown accustomed
to partialities,

that accretion
of absence, her black scarves
plucked from the top hat

one by one.
Then a miraculous
cumulus, removeless

completion.
Stoic mathematician,
efficient wizard,

reveal your secrets.
A lover
is going, some lover is always

going. Such curious
quadratics that
will not leave me whole.

It told the story of a runaway rose
that fled trellises, hedges, and the safety
of the master's shack for a life of abandon
in a town down the mountain, till the repressed
one-armed giantess packed her shears
and went to hunt. You recall the rest
only in shreds — the long travails of the giantess,
dark windy nights, a loud tavern where soldiers
bounced the blithe rose on their knees
and called it *Betty*. The inevitably violent end.
But what happened to that clarity of detail
you once knew? The thin book sported toothmarks
and a child's hieroglyphics, pages frayed
and smudged at the edge from too much turning.
You think the vanished facts of the story
must take their place in the continuing
erasures of your life: forgotten knowledge
and grammars, lost love, sensations and responses,
all heaped democratic in some dank
chaotic attic, with the occasional tantalizing
reminders to bait you, the way you remember,
years later, forgotten dreams at stoplights.
Or how as a child, carried drowsing from the car
by your father, you felt the prickly, solemn
pressure of a father's chest, and for the first time
felt yourself feeling, as if from a distance, and knew
you were somehow more than what was held.

Now you wonder that all you've forgotten
is already greater than what you contain,
a life conducted under skies
blunt and inexpressive as a giant's wrist.
Songs rise from the tavern to the valley
where vengeance waits, a fate sown
by the simple absence of a rowdy rose,
who at this moment carves initials in a table,
laughing, careless, as you struggle to picture
the specific, lurid end. Did the giantess
use the shears? Which arm was missing?

My dainty delinquents
twitch and fidget in their neat white beds.
O love I am coming

up the knotted trellis vine,
adoring. I sigh and I swoon,
I seize my lady's hand — sometimes

a girlish quiver, sometimes
a wedding band. I strew
blanched blossoms on the blossoming thighs.

The moon's luminous suitors
throb and rise. Time stutters, starts
again — time, time! Who's this

drowsing, hair tousled,
on the pillow? Did I
forget? It's true, I keep

no prizes. I am dapperest
in debt. Desire's
brief white waning is what

I die for. O breasts! white worlds
I plunder and divide. In the morning's
tumultuous parting, don't think me

heartless. Love, it is the sky's contusion
that jibes the bruise. Your need
cannot seduce me: the body

is my heart. Loss
can only loose me.
My hunger is my art.

Two men filched pumpkins from the grocery display.
It was late night, harsh. The' sprawled orange stack
preached of plenty while the moon
looked sarcastic. What loss! What lucid absence!
What roaming of suburban streets
with crazy globes. I thought of it next morning,
fixing oatmeal and coffee. Necessity. Surfeit.
I'd watched, one long year, my lover
feed his dying mother, the mashed food
laced with useless medications, the spoon
small in his hands. The old woman must have
barely known, stunned with age and her body's breaking.
The common slander of a failing heart,
her throat so choked with phlegm
even soft food could barely be taken.
But still her mouth sought each spoonful,
automatic and ready. What did she crave?
Peace or new life? Sometimes she called
for her father or long-dead friends. I remember
her faded eyes, the white hair oddly set.
Her mouth was thin and chipped with wrinkles,
it opened vaguely like a bird's or baby's
as my friend offered again and again the tiny bites.
There were stark hibiscus and a view of the inlet.
Early boaters and easy chatter and daily fear.

There was casual sunlight. We took meals
every morning. Nothing simple about it.
Something stolen. We must have known.

CHRONICLE

The sea's tedious soliloquies
drone and repeat
against the rinky-dink dock

where a tethered rowboat wrestles
an inexpert knot,
and wiry fishbones

stir in soggy air below
the shambled seawall not yet repaired.
Don't think *learn* or *listen* —

this speaks alone.
The jellyfish know,
splayed on waves, seeped

in seaweed, dividing,
joining. The starfish
know it, taut

in their mending dream.
Only *that one*
with its fists and its footsteps

wails regret: two legs,
one mind, and nothing
to be done.

O lost regeneration!
O saline amoeba! Elements
and gods have no words

for isolation,
though they're known to break
from the skull or thigh

a disquieting,
gray-eyed child
who bides her time.

II.

That time, you stood on my bed admiring the winter trees.

You said the sky's queer amber was the reflection of fallen snow.

What good is a sky, I might have asked, if it will not give us new blue distance, if it will only throw our loss back at us, shabby lens.

I folded the sheets, the thin mattress; across my apartment, you washed and dressed.

All winter, I grew pale and witchy, swatting erratic snowdrifts with my ancient, fraying broom.

I disproved your simplistic dualities, day by day.

A forgotten evening phone call, for example, will carve its resonant insult on mind and heart—but is that all?

What body is that, hunched and shaking at the kitchen table, oh so late?

Foolish Cartesian, your formula deceives you.

I recall your intelligent pleasure, much too well.

My eyes are strange gold, but no one's burned me as a witch yet. I would have flown my old broom right out of Syracuse, if it would have helped.

Dear sophist, dear sky, dear mirror. Did I love you for the madness you showed me? What could I see?

My broom wouldn't fly, I am no storybook witch;

nor Circe who turned men to swine, not that one either—

but faithful Calypso, that dispensable nymph,

whose name means, in the dead Greek language, *I am hiding.*

GLADIOLI

The elegant gladioli
in the flower store
do not even wish to grant me

their red regard.
They sense my history:
the defunct coleus,

the fraying, unwatered ferns,
the tragic succulent
root-bound in an infant pot.

I am changing,
I tell them. I am
a different woman.

They turn their flared faces
on stern regal necks.
O sheer

gash of fire,
brilliant sister,
forgive me.

LOVE (AMONG THE RUINS)

Conventional wisdom suggesting
collusion in forces opposing, meaning

I came to your house in a white dress
implying purity, promise, a random

forgiveness reserved for
the weak-willed carnivore

by the little girl who hurls her pin-striped
sack of peanuts at the elephant's head.

A shirred moon — regal, anemic — did preside.
Your guests flirted like flagrant doves or

compromised choirboys tippling
a weirder wine. Dancing —

or was it a grief-waltz never-ending,
despair such intimate

imprimatur, *do you, do I.*
Why lie,

the party was fissure,
our pale vernacular veering

into blur, a bed's-width of silence the only
reflex seeming

not reason but roar. Oasis
of redux in the garden where your

wife's plants passioned
as your moon-faced youngest acquired

blondness and hips. Not bitter
nor mythic, no, not mathematic,

no, not cervix nor cortex, no,
nor canny with words. Why lie,

I danced in a dress
of blue scribbles,

indecipherable script,
who might have been

white promise, collusion — coherent gown.

NO REGRETS

Edith Piaf, you are singing
for the strong ones, you are singing

for the chalk-faced believers in pagan faith,
as all bored bohemia

cocks its jaundiced ear. Your mythology
is smoke and shadow and rain-swept roads,

absolution in a black wool sweater,
feral lips. You leave nothing

for the winders of watches,
the dim, the shy ones,

the bearers and losers of umbrellas
on pure blue days.

Your voice on the ancient recording
is harsh and high,

a strident keening.
How did you come to

despise the given life?

FROM SHORE

The ocean goes, for fat miles.
When are we leaving? ask the children
as it swells and falls.
Such striving and failing
delights the amorous idiots at the railing
as they tipple cocktails on languorous ships.

The sea's advice to the lovelorn:
Obsession is tedium.
But how to ration
the pragmatic *tabula* of the sand
and all the warnings of a difficult season
to you, who grew up inland.

Immoderation is the seasonal edict: tulips spike from the earth
    with the force of the righteous, fist-sized,
uncompromising, unforgiving, barely natural ("the homespun
    surreal," I wrote my friend, "like David Lynch") on prim lawns
    the leisurely
envisioned for springtime. Note: seasons have meaning where the
    temperature changes (it is fresh life from sludge, it is renewal,
    it is strategic) —
these tulips aren't scribbles studded in notebooks, not crazy color
    on a ballerina spine,
they are burgeoned and blazoned, the pure indiscretion (for lack of
    restraint is the seasonal *jazz*),
are turbines and toxins. Zany. Malign. Are the clown's painted
    Bozo mouth on white foundation.
While at the backyard barbecue, I watched a man show a woman
    the fragile tulip innards
(the two might have been lovers) like one flower inside of another,
    so he said, and talk swayed
to the intrusion of deer in the suburbs, those devout tulip-eaters,
    the hunted at prey, as the sun creaked down
over houses, over apartments with their boxes of perfect *faux* tulips
    (for self-deception is the seasonal fashion, I am told), over the
    highway
with its lone deer sprawled on the curbside ("the usual complica-
    tions, usual hungers, usual roles"),

and over the balcony of the handsome restaurant downtown,
where two ceramic tulips posed austerely, careful, cold (you would
    not believe the science when he kissed me),
that must have been empty, that must have held nothing at all.

No good reflecting on what might have been
if I'd been different—no straying
after foreign flowers, no hunger
for bitter fruit. In the beginning—

such a child—I thought it punishment,
not fate. It is daylight I miss
mainly. What we are granted of sun here
is a dim relentless red. I wander

the reeking river, I pat
fat Cerberus on his many manic heads.
The moldy skiff makes its incessant
prompt arrivals, so efficient,

our dutiful Charon growling orders
from the prow. Huge-eyed, uncomprehending,
the new recruits stare round. Wives still
clutching their washing, wailing children,

soldiers blood-stained and battered
from the latest engagement.
Then that blessed briny sip, welcome
oblivion—they're blank as babies.

All night the shrieks of the tortured serenade
our marriage bed. Once it lulled
me rigid. For years after that
first celebrated rape,

I lay cold beneath his coldness,
stiff in his stiff embrace.
I'll give no prince to this kingdom.
That thing is dead.

For years, he broke me for it.
For years, I bled and bled.
That was then. Queen
of this blasphemous backwater,

I make my claim. On earth,
I am virginal abundance, fat and full.
Here, bony and empty, I straddle
my killer, my captor, my grief, my bane,

and tear and take
the torn lip, the raked neck, the aching thighs,
that will remind me
through the long black morning

I am alive.

Your Trotskyite friend poured his coffee
into the saucer. We and the waitress stared.
Perhaps it was proper decorum
in Detroit or wherever he was from.

Those long bickering breakfasts took the measure
of your small inebriate pretensions.
You said you were a difficult person.
Even on that point, I wouldn't agree.

You spoke of Trotsky's assassination
in the Mexican sun, by hired guns
of Stalin and the USA. It was
whispered conspiracy in a breathless cabana.

It was tapped phone lines on company pay.
The Fourth International and world revolution.
You said, you'd said you were a difficult
person. I might agree.

You said you'd worked in factories
and knew things. Secret files
in gray buildings. I should see. You
only hit me twice. You said you'd told me

you were a difficult person. Everyone
was out to get you. I'd see.
You wanted to change the world.
It was something on which we agreed.

THE CASE

Old wolf, I said,
leave a tatter
for my family,
a scrap, a rag,
a bone, a button — something
to bury.
          Because, I said,
I've chased
the fast fox from
the henhouse, and twisted
the livid blossoms
from failing stems,
mercy, spare a rag,
a bone, a button,
for my family.

And because, I said, I sang
the names of saints
on Sunday, and lay
with another woman's
husband Monday eve, leave
a scrap, a rag,
a bone, a button —
to bury.

And he said:
It will take
whatever it is given. It will
be still.

EVENING

The child calling and calling
his lost dog home on the long
suburban block, doesn't know he is part
of a peculiar orchestration,
along with traffic, and the predictable
humming of my fridge, and the tick
of the clock still not set back
from daylight savings — a music
specific to a private
kitchen view, in the unfolding
dimensions of a sepia twilight
from which comes, again
and again, the high far note
of the child in his chanting,
so natural and knowing that it
might happen every dusk,
as if loss were an inevitable
condition of nightfall,
spread from streets and houses
to an open, barren hill, and to
the hulking, enigmatic water-
tower, bulbous, beneath which
a frail white dog must be asleep.

PRIMITIVES

Every heaven is a star put on
like a tin crown by the modest
at New Year's time when we neither forget
nor depart from the wreckage of whose
torn gown there are lamps to light
but in nowise the candle.

, , ,

Most fearful unrooted, a cruel hand
plucked you, overnight the sea sheds
degrees for the radiance of able
stars and night fish to guide
shadowy sailors whose pale hearts hum
in this we were wise in this there is reason.

, , ,

Sags and catches, its breath
in a rage of feints do you say
never the first word I give old hats
to new heads it never fails being
more of a demon than a dream in my
wealth of unwinter I will always sing.

, , ,

Dropped she has given best grief
to the blessed our hands two stones
the lip is formula the eye control
have I given old wealth like a spoken
word when they forget never its first
light candle blue and red.

                    ▾ ▾ ▾

Is infinity like this is my answer
to the dividends and dropped ones
you need money like a fish needs flint
though failing my oath in an acrobatic
pact, no one gives to the graces their
faintest remembrance of face.

                    ▾ ▾ ▾

Not having owned not having striven
not having wrecked not having drawn
like a wraith in a ring or a muzzle
on a skeleton will we dream our new worth
feeds like a moth on fibers from
the drawer unopened the stitch unstrung.

                    ▾ ▾ ▾

That this were my mirth full of promise
elides the twin seasons in a song
not full of merit but more in its
thrilled composure a new move never
be the prize you pivot think
this is poverty this is caress.

                    ▾ ▾ ▾

As for the moon she mines you
like a wealth your hands pale hands
give a new sequence saying
more than a grace grown fatal
as we are naming suspects placing
every stream every tree every stone.

COMBUSTION

In my wrist
veins twist
blue flames

to the heart's nest,
a torqued force,
centrifugal,

spinning out
from any center
it finds. It burns,

it blinds, it takes
life from
my life, flared

fist, jealous
furnace, assassin
reeling in fevered

rings. My angels dance
on the tips of matches.
They have no wings.

III.

THE ROSE GARDEN

A polka strikes up in the old gazebo
where the grown-ups and children have gathered
because it is summer and the snow is gone.
The banks of roses

are in full ecstasy today,
having conquered
soporific winter one more year.
We know the new strains

by their namesakes:
movie stars, couturiers —
more fitting, in their flash,
than any rational Latin.

Young and confident,
we hold hands and stroll the footpaths,
bending to stroke
the plush plumage, to learn each

profligate message: *tell me
you love me for we will
never marry.* O botanists,
engineers of excess,

what have you done?
It is summer in Syracuse
and the snow is gone.
In the gazebo, two gray-haired women

dance, the one who's leading
wears a straw hat with a blue band
and flowered sprig.
Confident and young,

we hold hands and watch, we wonder
what power drives us
to bow to every blossom,
even the scentless.

DR. FEELGOOD

Got to be a gimcrack somewhere could gauge the scope of it.
Whole world whole hips whole crisis kind of thing.
Some hottentot madonna
not minding her p's and q's like in the old days.

But the lab found only
a few cells gone bad and a gee-whiz kind of quiet,
one custom-made prison — oasis in a bird cage —
yellowed sheet music (accompaniment for organ).

Mind over motion. So the melody goes.
And a black feather boa. Useless for soaring.
Immutable. Elements. Loose a. Blue sun.
Untranslatable. Paeans. In a guttural. Tongue.

THE PREGNANT LADY PLAYING TENNIS

The pregnant lady playing tennis
bobs on her toes at the court's left side,
raises the green ball high, and sets it

spinning. Then moving in circles
of deliberate size, she returns the lob
with the same giddy grace. In the quiet glide

of the lady playing tennis,
there's a knowledge of speeds and angles,
arcs and aims. From the other courts,

the players watch, dismayed, half-fearing
for the safety of the lady playing tennis,
half-wishing this odd distraction shut away.

Tennis, they notice, is a dangerous game.
But the ovals close
on the lady playing tennis, as if

the tight-knit mesh of her racket
were a magnet, with the ball
a perfect pole veering home. Watching

each hard-shot lob clear the net,
the pregnant lady playing tennis
braces in the pure sensation of her game,

in her body's stretch and haul, and plants
a crazy slam past the net: past the lines,
past the out zone, past the court's steel network wall.

Now, though, the wind lifts in a thousand particular stories.
Old notes gather and scatter. We're not ourselves. Liking well the
separation. You said you needed to see a man about a something —
"change of heart" or "raw deal," I can't recall.

I'd like to be better, but I'm short on time. (The river running
backwards, as predicted.) There are balloons and children shooting
pistols, dozens of questions. Implausible, natural. Cannon fire . . .
no, a kid with a bongo.

Now who's not not seeming. And a world of intentions teeters
like a cheap globe! Gather. Scatter. On the promenade wall, a gull
inspects a ribcage. Necessity, old comrade, tags along.

CHEMISTRY

Having lived with the lightning,
the arson was easy. Aftermath

and a few chuckles for the seriousness
assumed by firemen and witnesses.

What were you expecting, a tango
for breakfast among the torched remnants,

sparks assessed by duration and length?
I go with it. I'm easy.

Dropped from the sky
by a glider bearing brimstone,

original oracle. Have a heart,
I said—take two, they're flexible.

Fold to a crumb in your pocket,
but love is like that. An expanding

molecule when you need it. Oxygen
odorless and tasteless but less

essential. Do we buy this
periodic table giving the lie

elements are orderly
when we take the blank spots

to our hearts — a pale implosion,
an amplitude given — as love

lies down among us, becoming
wonder and fire, levitating mass.

WHITE LILY

Gnomish in its rounded hunch
of greeny folds, three-fourths of the year
it resembles a weed. Now spring's

unseasonable heat
brings vindication. Trumpet
over frilled, frail trumpet

spills its bone-white notes
in April air. Below, in shadow —
shrunken, overawed — skulks

the novice rosebush
we rooted in the fall. This
spendthrift, who's squandered

brilliant buds for months,
today knows the earthy weight
of morning-after. Our double

hibiscus, also, pinkly plumed,
succumbed to a plumber's truck
that veered too soon. But the lily

in her straight ascetic's
rigid pose, white as the ember
of a low, enduring fire

takes her pleasure like
the wife of the pastor
come to bed — prim in her cotton frock

throughout the day, precise
in her firm instructions
to the maid, who cradled

in the rough caress of muslin sheets
bares her stoic shoulders to the room
and seizes in her strong white legs

the truant moon.

Never having owned
the sweet-limbed cherry-cheeked
dolls of a certain age, whose
puffed pinafores brushed
artistically dimpled knees, or
the two-dimensional cutouts pressed
in a detailed dress, I instead
built the non-representational
from Legos, whose stark rectangles
gripped in a fist
cut perfect lines, or from Tinker Toys,
whose wheels and poles must have
been integrals unaided, all painted
typical, hubristic, bleak
primary shades, a child's tactile
grasp on the essential,
forming creations based
on that simplest equation,
protruding part set
to hole, male to female,
the pure, the absolute,
the abstract, the elemental,
with no slightest correlation
to anything human,
the useless geometric
acts, the strange inventions,

which from a shifting twenty years
distance cannot teach me
how I left the angular
unpeopled landscapes alone.

SHIPWRECK POEM

I

Navigation's gone haywire. Who's to blame?
Night blacker than chartless depth

and above us
the astonishing unimpeachable stars!

and pale my sister
votive Pole Star, oracular tear.

In no dream of safety
do we live — bed and wave —

as I lost faith to be here.
It was love that shattered my compass —

searching room to room in the storm,
and you gone, the new moon

blind with delusions, the high deck
reeking of whale oil and tallow,

imagined latitudes,
instruments and digits,

the mast splintered
in a rogue wave, the flotsam crying

This is the life you made.

II
The sea deposits debris
carelessly, as though it could be

the whole story, clue held
to eye to tongue to ear,

wonderful offal! Ungraspable,
the whole deep havoc

adheres to the hands of the Collector,
who would be clear

as shore lights in summer.
What I left to be here —

certain firmament and fair wind,
for spiky trophies and

attenuating shore.
O lord I spoke too soon

of love and the wondrous.
Outside my skin it was always

bad religion.
The same story:

a child's yellow shovel
and a world to dig in.

Clear as shore lights in summer,
forward not back

swims the woman
I *will* be, summoned

not with the compass, *not* with the map.

SCARECROW

Love loves the time when the road ends.
When the immaculate fever
comes down, loving the distance,
and the luminous wheat in high wind
and the apples.

A man is not a scarecrow, he
breathes and beats at the wind
with a pair of hands.
Throw an apple at him, he takes it, he bites it.
He knows a thing or two

about the country where *you* live,
country of weather,
country of bitten fruit.
He abides with crows
and the harvest, the restless

rifling of acres, evanescent green.
The horizon ignites
where *you* live. Your skirt
full of apples
and dirty. It will not

end well.

DAFFODILS

O my mimics, my gangly girls,
morning came quickly
with blushes and exits,

you left without saying
goodbye, without warning, Sonia
and Nina, by moonlight leaping

white steps to the station, Nina
and Anya, you left
no addresses, pointe shoes

in your handbags, lipstick askew,
Anya, Maria, the conductor called
Dreaming, the conductor called *Dancing,*

the conductor called *Far,*
you saw towers and bridges, Maria
and Katya, horizons and oceans,

gowns and perfumes
(by moonlight leaping
white steps to the station), dear Katya,

Marina, you left no addresses,
no notes or instructions,
no map and no route, the conductor

called *Farther*, and we gaze
from the platform, to your pale eyes,
Marina, Sophia, on the train.

SEASONAL

Much melting, and crows close to home.
Snow giving its fingerprints this March morning.
If I could, I would take your arm
in the manner of our European forebears,
linked elbows, fist pressed close to the heart,
singing songs to the springtime, singing old songs.
It would be this much to give to the world,
to the dead in the ground who need consoling, need consoling.
It would be this much to give to the world
which is not like a boot in the face, but a blessing.
The wordless birches rise up, a pure promise, but it is
early, the day collects in puddles, you are far off.
And remembering noise in the wind, and remembering.
Your eyes which are paler than sleep
kissed from the forehead of one who is still dreaming.
If I could, I would take your arm.
Then the crow in the pine would know us, saying
These are the ones who knew so little, all this time.

IN REHEARSAL

The mustachioed stagehand is striking the sets
again, while the man in the red satin gown
stamps a rapacious tango
through the tremulous hall.

I can't come home, darling,
I have to work, we are preparing
the next silly musical
with its pratfalls and its swoons.

I'm in the box office. I'm selling tickets.
I count the dollars. I write reports.
Yes, it's tempting, when you drop by
with your cakes and cookies

and hazel eyes, but *please*,
this is business,
that famous artist is painting flats
with magnificent scarlet ballrooms,

with foaming oceans, and gallant ships.
I have no time now
for everyday illusions.
Please go home. I'm working,

I'm phoning jugglers,
fencing masters, dancing bears,
breeders of pugs and Pekingese,
red-haired triplets, snake charmers,

fire-walkers and shamans, ferocious cats.
Oh, don't be glum, love, there's always
someday—leave what you brought me,
then run along. I hear the clink of foils

in the hallway (we are so busy), and our leading
lady shouting *The Spaniards are landing!*
The Spaniards are landing! as you
pass me sweetbreads through unbreakable glass.

REGRET LYRIC

As though there were too much,
a white birch splayed chiaroscuro,
a new mouth and a rough wind
and the red ghost recollection

needing time —
a little space please —
the anxious wilderness
patterns and flashes on

the roadbend named "too late"
what we walk toward,
evading your issuance, lord,
in wide morning, leaving wing.

Snow is falling, in a world much like this one, the wood dark, sky
    heavier — moon turned to stone — and the path

inscribed, active, where the stepper beveled in Goretex and Thermax
    attends the still navigable darkness (much like this)

whelped from warmth like kisses — collaborator with a strawberry lip —
    and fresh snow topples from a bough —

but what do I know? Accepting the legends, reading the clues,
    the deer tracks stamped in pairs, the timid drifters,

fifty inches of snow the going myth for this Thursday's blizzard,
    burying town and city in chilly brimstone, now the moon

hoisted like harlequin, a hoedown, a version of freedom to go on
    or stay in, attenuated ember, tin token, phony star,

and the wood like a womb, and the crow like a weapon, and the pine
    like a guardian, and the birch like bone,

it is inclement weather, analogy losing its manners, where memory
    scrambled in the trees and missed a beat,

temperature, fever, thermometer, scar, injury, accident, a burden,
    a pleasure, a tremor much like this,

who would be the tall one turning the tables, and the dervish
    in the high chair, and the pale one tamping the lid down,

and the saved one and the lost one, the one on the path, one
    foundered in a snowdrift, and the one with the ravingest eye,
    revising

the first photographs of earth, all wispy cloudlets and ingenuous
    blue, as you tender your scared stretch of life

like a blessing — moon broke to blossom! — and (the mind leaves
    the body on the path) keen and shine.